I Heard God Laughing

I Heard God Laughing

Renderings of Hafiz

by Daniel Ladinsky

Consulting Editor
Henry S. Mindlin

Hafiz

Shams-ud-din Muhammad Hafiz (*c.* 1320–1389), though little known in the Western world, is the most beloved poet of Persia (Iran). To Persians, the poems of Hafiz are not "classical literature" from a remote past, but cherished wisdom from a dear and intimate friend. The special gift of this friend is a poetry unique in world literature, a poetry that celebrates every expression of love in the universe.

The lyrics of Hafiz overflow with a profound appreciation of the beauty and richness of life when seen through the eyes of love. With unerring insight, he explores the feelings and motives associated with every level of love, tracing each nuance of emotion in depth and detail. His poetry outlines the stages of the mystic's "path of love" — that journey of inner unfolding in which love dissolves personal boundaries and limitations to join larger processes of growth and transformation. Through these processes, human love becomes divine love and the lover merges ultimately with the source and goal of all love, which Hafiz calls the Divine Beloved.

International Standard Book Number: 0-915828-18-9
Library of Congress Catalog Card Number: 96-67524
First printing, 1996
Second printing, 1997
Third printing, 1999
Fourth printing, 2000
Fifth printing, 2001
Sixth printing, 2002

Printed in the United States of America
by Paris Printing, Novato, CA

Cover illustration by Diane Cobb
Book design by Sidney Davenport

Sufism Reoriented
1300 Boulevard Way
Walnut Creek, California 94595

Contents

Releasing the Spirit of Hafiz

My work with Hafiz began on an early morning walk in the countryside of central India, on a beautiful tree-lined road that leads to a place called Meherazad. This small, private residential community near the city of Ahmednagar was the home of the great spiritual Master Avatar Meher Baba until his passing in 1969. A small group of the Master's lifelong companions continue to live and work there, surrounded by a remarkable atmosphere of love.

I was walking with a man whom I have come to know as a teacher, a brother and a friend, a man who had been a member of the Master's circle since the late 1930s. On this particular morning, we were discussing Hafiz, who was Meher Baba's favorite poet. Though Hafiz lived in the fourteenth century, his verses are still immensely popular throughout the Near East and India. His insight and compassion, his subtle, expressive language and his deep reverence for beauty in all its forms have made him a favorite poet of lovers, and especially of lovers of God. The Sufis say that Hafiz loved so fully and so well that he became the living embodiment of Love. Meher Baba called him "a Perfect Master and a perfect poet."

Poetry was in the air at Meherazad that week. The day before our walk, we had listened to a program of marvelous English translations of Rumi, another Persian master poet, who lived a century before Hafiz. Now, as we walked, I turned to my mentor and companion and candidly said, "Compared to those splendid versions of Rumi we heard yesterday, the poetry of Hafiz can appear so *pale* in English! How can this be, when Meher Baba says that Hafiz is such a great poet?" He replied, "Baba has said it is because no one has yet properly translated

Hafiz!" As soon as he said that, I was surprised to hear myself say, "I can do that!" That night, though I did not (and do not) know the Persian language, I wrote my first version of a Hafiz poem, working from a literal English translation.

For hundreds of years, people have struggled to find ways to reflect in English the sweetness and profundity of Hafiz's poetry. Some translators have tried to reproduce the rhythm, meter and rhyme of the original Persian, often bending and twisting English into strange and unfamiliar configurations to do so. Such careful efforts to honor the *form* of the poetry can sometimes ignore or violate the *spirit* of Hafiz—a spirit of infinite tenderness and compassion, of great exuberance, joy and laughter, of ecstatic love and fervent longing for his Beloved, and of wonder and delight at the divine splendor of the universe. I wanted to find ways to release that spirit in our own language.

The poems of Hafiz are mostly short love songs called *ghazals,* each one about the length of a sonnet. Scholars disagree about the exact number of poems that can be authenticated, but there are no more than eight hundred. Compared to Rumi and others, this is a tiny body of work. However, Hafiz created his poetry in a way that permits many kinds of interpretation. Persian is a flexible and mutable language, and Hafiz was an absolute master of it. Persian-speaking friends say that in some of his poems each *word* can have seven or eight shades of meaning and a variety of interpretations. A single couplet can be translated many different ways, and each one would be "right."

I quickly discovered that even in English, a single Hafiz poem, often a single couplet, could be approached from many points of view. A single stanza of Hafiz could generate whole families of independent poems in English, each exploring some aspect of the original. One might call the results "renderings" or renditions of Hafiz, rather than "translations." To "render" an artistic work means to interpret, to express, to realize. The word can also mean "surrendering" and "yielding" —in this case, opening to the guidance of the spirit contained within the poetry. Thus my poems are not "translations" in any traditional sense. They are not intended to be literal or scholarly or even "accurate." But I hope they are True—faithful to the living spirit of this divine poet.

These "renderings" are based on a remarkable translation of Hafiz by H. Wilberforce Clarke, originally published in 1891. I work from a beautiful two-volume, 1011-page edition of Clarke's work, recently republished in Iran. I also borrow and shape ideas and thoughts from a few of the many other available translations of Hafiz. A Select Bibliography of sources is included at the end of this book along with information about the life of Hafiz and the background of his poetry.

It is my understanding that when Hafiz created his poems, he often spoke them or sang them spontaneously and his companions wrote the verses down later. Even if one does not know Persian, it is easy to appreciate the rhythm and music of his "playful verse" when one hears it recited aloud. Many of his poems were set to popular tunes, and they are still sung now, six hundred years later, all over the East. Several of these English renderings have already inspired new songs of Hafiz for the West by many gifted musicians. I'm sure Hafiz would be delighted. These poems are meant to be recited, sung, even happily shouted—if it won't disturb the neighbors too much!

What can I say to my dear Master, Meher Baba, for all his help and guidance? Whatever truth, beauty, laughter and charm you may find here, I would say is a gift from him, the Avatar.

May these poems inspire us to give the great gift of kindness—to ourselves and to others.

Daniel Ladinsky
February 25, 1996

May these poems help reveal the Truth
Of God's Divine Playfulness and Light
And His Sublime Intimacy with us.

Poetic Conventions

Hafiz uses a few Persian literary devices that may initially confuse Western readers:

In some poems, Hafiz is like a playwright who is acting all the parts: the lover, the disciple, the Master and Guide, the voice of God, sometimes even the reader. Often *I, you, he* or *she,* and *Hafiz* refer to the same person.

He frequently includes his name, Hafiz, in at least one stanza. This was a method of "signing" the poem, as one might sign a letter to a friend or as an artist might sign a painting.

Hafiz uses a technical vocabulary to write about stages of spiritual unfolding. Fortunately, his images are so vivid and real that one does not need to understand the mysticism to recognize the experience. In essence, all mysticism deals with processes of love and the ways in which one joins God through love. For Hafiz, the focus of love is often a Master of Love, described as a Luminous Figure, *Pir* (Friend), or sometimes the Tavern-keeper, the one who pours Love's Wine. The Master puts the student on intimate terms with God, who is called the Friend, the Beloved, the Beautiful One.

You Are with the Friend Now

Hafiz describes some of the preparations required for the inner "Journey of Love." He urges us to let go of habitual negative attitudes and unnecessary attachments, which only weigh us down. To make this Journey, we must be light, happy and free to go Dancing!

"I wish I could show you,
When you are lonely or in darkness,

The Astonishing Light

Of your own Being!"

A Divine Invitation

You have been invited to meet
The Friend.

No one can resist a Divine Invitation.

That narrows down all our choices
To just two:

We can come to God
Dressed for Dancing,

Or

Be carried on a stretcher
To God's Ward.

You Don't Have to Act Crazy Anymore

You don't have to act crazy anymore—
We all know you were good at that.

Now retire, my dear,
From all that hard work you do

Of bringing pain to your sweet eyes and heart.

Look in a clear mountain mirror—
See the Beautiful Ancient Warrior
And the Divine elements
You always carry inside

That infused this Universe with sacred Life
So long ago

And join you Eternally
With all Existence—with God!

We Should Talk about This Problem

There is a Beautiful Creature
Living in a hole you have dug.

So at night
I set fruit and grains
And little pots of wine and milk
Beside your soft earthen mounds,

And I often sing.

But still, my dear,
You do not come out.

I have fallen in love with Someone
Who hides inside you.

We should talk about this problem—

Otherwise,
I will never leave you alone.

And Applaud

Once a young man came to me and said,

"Dear Master,
I am feeling strong and brave today,
And I would like to know the truth
About all of my—attachments."

And I replied,

"Attachments?
Attachments!

Sweet Heart,
Do you really want me to speak to you
About all your attachments,

When I can see so clearly
You have built, with so much care,
Such a great brothel
To house all of your pleasures.

You have even surrounded the whole damn place
With armed guards and vicious dogs
To protect your desires

So that you can sneak away
From time to time
And try to squeeze light
Into your parched being
From a source as fruitful
As a dried date pit
That even a bird
Is wise enough to spit out.

Your attachments! My dear,
Let's not speak of those,

For Hafiz understands the sufferings
Of your heart.

Hafiz knows
The torments and the agonies
That every mind on the way to Annihilation in the Sun
Must endure.

So at night in my prayers I often stop
And ask a thousand angels to join in
And Applaud,

And Applaud
Anything,
Anything in this world
That can bring your heart comfort!"

Manic Screaming

We should make all spiritual talk
Simple today:

God is trying to sell you something,
But you don't want to buy.

That is what your suffering is:

Your fantastic haggling,
Your manic screaming over the price!

My Brilliant Image

One day the sun admitted,

I am just a shadow.
I wish I could show you
The Infinite Incandescence *(Tej)*

That has cast my brilliant image!

I wish I could show you,
When you are lonely or in darkness,

The Astonishing Light

Of your own Being!

Cast All Your Votes for Dancing

I know the voice of depression
Still calls to you.

I know those habits that can ruin your life
Still send their invitations.

But you are with the Friend now
And look so much stronger.

You can stay that way
And even bloom!

Keep squeezing drops of the Sun
From your prayers and work and music
And from your companions' beautiful laughter.

Keep squeezing drops of the Sun
From the sacred hands and glance of your Beloved
And, my dear,
From the most insignificant movements
Of your own holy body.

Learn to recognize the counterfeit coins
That may buy you just a moment of pleasure,
But then drag you for days
Like a broken man
Behind a farting camel.

You are with the Friend now.
Learn what actions of yours delight Him,
What actions of yours bring freedom
And Love.

Whenever you say God's name, dear pilgrim,
My ears wish my head was missing
So they could finally kiss each other
And applaud all your nourishing wisdom!

O keep squeezing drops of the Sun
From your prayers and work and music
And from your companions' beautiful laughter

And from the most insignificant movements
Of your own holy body.

Now, sweet one,
Be wise.
Cast all your votes for Dancing!

Come to My House

Hafiz introduces himself as Companion and Guide, Friend and Lover. He invites us to share his life, his wine and his heart, to see ourselves and the world through his eyes. If we didn't know better, we would think he was courting us — and perhaps he is!

"If your cellar is empty,
This whole Universe
Could drink forever
From mine!"

What Happens

What happens when your soul
Begins to awaken
Your eyes
And your heart
And the cells of your body
To the great Journey of Love?

First there is wonderful laughter
And probably precious tears

And a hundred sweet promises
And those heroic vows
No one can ever keep.

But still God is delighted and amused
You once tried to be a saint.

What happens when your soul
Begins to awake in this world

To our deep need to love
And serve the Friend?

O the Beloved
Will send you
One of His wonderful, wild companions—

Like Hafiz.

Someone Who Can Kiss God

Come to my house late at night —
Do not be shy.
Hafiz will be barefoot and dancing.

I will be
In such a grand and generous mood!

Come to my door at any hour,
Even if your eyes
Are frightened by my light.
My heart and arms are open
And need no rest —
They will always welcome you.

Come in, my dear,
From that harsh world
That has rained elements of stone
Upon your tender face.

Every soul
Should receive a toast from us
For bravery!

Bring all the bottles of wine you own
To this divine table — the earth
We share.

If your cellar is empty,
This whole Universe
Could drink forever
From mine!

Let's dine tonight with exquisite music.
I might even hire angels
To play —just for you.

Look!
Hidden beneath your feet
Is a Luminous Stage
Where we are meant to rehearse
Our Eternal Dance!

And what is the price of my Divine Instruction?
What could I ask of you?

All I could ever want
Is that
You have the priceless company
Of Someone
Who can Kiss God,

That you have the priceless gift
Of becoming a servant to the Friend!

Come to my window, dear world —
Why ever be shy?

Look inside my playful Verse,
For Hafiz is Barefoot and Dancing
And in such a Grand and Generous —
In such a Fantastic Mood.

Would You Think It Odd?

Would you think it odd if Hafiz said,

"I am in love with every church
And mosque
And temple
And any kind of shrine

Because I know it is there
That people say the different names
Of the One God."

Would you tell your friends
I was a bit strange if I admitted

I am indeed in love with every mind
And heart and body.

O I am sincerely
Plumb crazy
About your every thought and yearning
And limb

Because, my dear,
I know
That it is through these

That you search for Him.

Someone Calls Your Name

Someone calls your name in a crowd,
And Hafiz, too, begins to look around.

You receive a piece of
Hoped-for foreign mail,
And Hafiz, too,
Becomes so excited to open it.

You lie down with a lover
After many days apart,
And Hafiz will close his eyes
When things get bare and moving,
If you ask.

My dear, there is something
You should think about and that is:

If just an old sweeper of the Tavern
Can truly be so near
And intimate with you,
How extraordinary
Must be your relationship
With — *God, God, God!*

The Jeweler

If a naive and desperate man
Brings a precious stone
To the only jeweler in town,
Wanting to sell it,

The jeweler's eyes
Will begin to play a game,
Like most eyes in the world when they look at you.

The jeweler's face will stay calm.
He will not want to reveal the stone's true value,
But to hold the man captive to fear and greed
While he calculates
The value of the transaction.

But one moment with me, my dear,
Will show you
That there is nothing,
Nothing
Hafiz wants from you.

When you sit before a Master like me,
Even if you are a drooling mess,
My eyes sing with Excitement—

They see your Divine Worth.

Saints Bowing in the Mountains

Do you know how beautiful you are?

I think not, my dear.

For as you talk of God,
I see great parades with wildly colorful bands
Streaming from your mind and heart,
Carrying wonderful and secret messages
To every corner of this world.

I see saints bowing in the mountains
Hundreds of miles away
To the wonder of sounds
That break into light
From your most common words.

Speak to me of your mother,
Your cousins and your friends.

Tell me of squirrels and birds you know.
Awaken your legion of nightingales —
Let them soar wild and free in the sky

And begin to sing to God.
Let's all begin to sing to God!

Do you know how beautiful you are?

I think not, my dear,

Yet Hafiz
Could set you upon a Stage
And worship you forever!

Exquisitely Woven

Wayfarer,
Your body is my prayer carpet,

For I can see in your eyes

That you are exquisitely woven
With the finest silk and wool

And that Pattern upon your soul
Has the signature of God

And all your moods and colors of love
Come from His Divine vats of dye and
Gold.

Wayfarer,
Your body is my shrine.

If you had the eyes of a *Pir*,

You would see Hafiz
Kneeling by your side,

Humming playful tunes
And shedding joyful tears

Upon your wondrous hidden Crown.

The Moon Is Also Busy

I bow to God in gratitude,
And I find the moon is also busy
Doing the same.

I bow to God in great happiness,
And I learn from where the suns
And the children
And my heart
All borrow their Light.

I bow to the Friend in deep reverence
And discover a marvelous secret carried in the air:

This whole Universe is just as blessed
And divinely crazed as I,
And just as lost in this Wonderful Holy Dance.

My dear,
After such a long, long journey,
God has made another soul
Free!

Now all Hafiz wants to do
Is open a beautiful Tavern
Where this Sacred Wine
Of God's Truth, Knowledge and Love
Is forever and ever
Freely offered to you.

O bow to God in gratitude,
And some day
You will see how
The moon is also busy doing the same.

We All Sit in God's Classroom

Hafiz tells us that Love's Journey unfolds through every process of life. Divine principles are constantly being demonstrated all around us. We cannot learn them through words or books or limited systems of human values. Hafiz says God is fully known only through love, which accepts *everything*. Love reveals the Universe as a cosmic playground where every thing and being participates in a single, magnificent Game.

"God has shouted 'Yes! Yes! Yes!'
To every luminous movement in Existence."

For a While

We have all come to the right place.
We all sit in God's classroom.

Now,
The only thing left for us to do, my dear,

Is to stop
Throwing spitballs for a while.

Why Carry?

Hafiz,
Why carry a whole load of books
Upon your back
Climbing this mountain,
When tonight,
Just a few thoughts of God
Will light the holy fire.

Someone Should Start Laughing

I have a thousand brilliant lies
For the question:

How are you?

I have a thousand brilliant lies
For the question:

What is God?

If you think that the Truth can be known
From words,

If you think that the Sun and the Ocean

Can pass through that tiny opening
Called the mouth,

O someone should start laughing!

Someone should start wildly Laughing—
Now!

A Golden Compass

Forget every idea of right and wrong
Any classroom ever taught you

Because
An empty heart, a tormented mind,
Unkindness, jealousy and fear

Are always the testimony
You have been completely fooled!

Turn your back on those
Who would imprison your wondrous spirit
With deceit and lies.

Come, join the honest company
Of the King's beggars—
Those gamblers, scoundrels and divine clowns
And those astonishing fair courtesans
Who need Divine Love every night.

Come, join the courageous
Who have no choice
But to bet their entire world
That indeed,
Indeed, God is Real.

I will lead you into the Circle
Of the Beloved's cunning thieves,
Those playful royal rogues—
The ones you can trust for true guidance—
Who can aid you
In this Blessed Calamity of life.

Hafiz,
Look at the Perfect One
At the Circle's Center:

He Spins and Whirls like a Golden Compass,
Beyond all that is Rational,

To show this dear world

That Everything,
Everything in Existence
Does point to God.

Zero

Zero
Is where the Real Fun starts.

There's too much counting
Everywhere else!

Circles

The moon is most happy
When it is full.

And the sun always looks
Like a perfectly minted gold coin

That was just Polished
And placed in flight
By God's playful Kiss.

And so many varieties of fruit
Hang plump and round

From branches that seem like a Sculptor's hands.

I see the beautiful curve of a pregnant belly
Shaped by a soul within,

And the Earth itself,
And the planets and the Spheres—

I have gotten the hint:

There is something about circles
The Beloved likes.

Hafiz,
Within the Circle of a Perfect One

There is an Infinite Community
Of Light.

The Great Secret

God was full of Wine last night,
So full of Wine

That He let a great secret slip.

He said:

There is no man on this earth
Who needs a pardon from Me —

For there is really no such thing,
No such thing
As Sin!

The Beloved has gone completely Wild —
He has poured Himself into me!

I am Blissful and Drunk and Overflowing.

Dear world,
Draw life from my Sweet Body.

Dear wayfaring souls,
Come drink your fill of liquid rubies,
For God has made my heart
An Eternal Fountain!

Wayfarer

Wayfarer,

Your whole mind and body have been tied
To the foot of the Divine Elephant
With a thousand golden chains.

Now, begin to rain intelligence and compassion
Upon all your tender, wounded cells

And realize the profound absurdity
Of thinking

That you can ever go Anywhere
Or do Anything

Without God's will.

Of Course Things Like That Can Happen

Once God made love to a great saint
Who had a hairy belly.

Of course things like that can happen!

And it was a surprise
Only to the novice on the path
When the saint's stomach began to swell
Just like a woman's.

Weeks went by, then months.
The saint's cheeks
Turned into beautiful roses.
He became like a young bride
Who was carrying a holy child,
And his gratitude was speechless.
But his eyes shone
Like two planets making love.

The town began to stand outside his house
At night,

For it had come to the attention of the faithful
That as the moon passed by on its round,
It would sometimes bend over and kiss his roof!

Of course things like that can happen.

Life went on
Amidst the other ten thousand wonders:
Whiskers and weeds and trees and charming babies
Kept emerging.
People and cattle and bees worked side by side,
All sweetly humming.
And, come lunch,
All dined on the same Mysterious
Divine manna of nourishing Love—
Disguised in a thousand shapes, colors and forms.

Galaxies gave away their ingenious ideas
And told us of their private body functions.
So man, too,
Eats, burps and excretes more worlds.

How is it that invisible thoughts can lift heavy matter
And build cities and armies and altars?

All contain a Hidden Strategy
To be transformed again
Into Divine Music and Love and Light!

The sun rolls through
The sky meadows every day,
And a billion cells run
To the top of a leaf to scream and applaud
And smash things in their joy.

Of course things like that can happen.

Rivers stay up all night and chant;
Luminous fish jump out of the water
Spitting emeralds at all talk of Heaven
Being anywhere else but— Right Here!

Clouds pull each other's pants down
And point and laugh.

O my dear,
Of course things like that can happen.

For all is written within the Mind
To help and instruct the dervish
In dance and romance and prayer.

The stars get clearly drunk
And crazy at night
And throw themselves
Across the sky.

Only an insane being or compound
Is not going mad with excitement
At this Wonderful Performance by God!

And still,
Light stretches its arms
Open even more
And shouts to you, because you are His lover,
To forget your harsh actions of the past
And just Dance!

Look! Angels and flowers
Are playing hooky in graveyards,
Laughing and rolling naked on cool stones.

Why go to sleep tonight
Exhausted from the folly of ignorance,

When even the Beloved is Drunk
And is doing wonderful, ecstatic somersaults
And is giving wild lessons between the sheets
And between His handstands
All up and down the Tavern floor and ceiling!

Indeed,
Indeed, things like that can happen.

A few days
Before the delivery of God's baby,
The saint had to visit a city close by
Where few knew of him.

He was walking unnoticed past a mosque,
And the shouts of God's lovers
Happened to fill the air, calling,

"Allah, Allah! Where are you?
Where are You, Beautiful One?"

And the child in the womb of the Master
Could not remain silent and shouted back,
In an astounding voice,

I am Here!
I am Here — dear world!

The crowd in the mosque became frantic,
And they picked up shoes, clubs and stones.
You know what then happened —
The story becomes grim.

But the moon cannot hold a grudge.
It still stops by some nights
And leans over this gentle earth, as over a crib,
And gives a full, wet kiss.

For the moon knows
That God is always amorous —

He will never stop making Love,

For the Truth has been Divinely Conceived
Deeply within each of us.

O Hafiz,
Look at the Splendor of God's Grace:
The Sun has been planted in a thousand furrows
Across every soul's brow.

Of course, my dear,
Everything God and I say
Can Happen!

The Only One

From man's perspective
In this intricate game of love,

It is so easy to become confused
And think you are the do-er.

But from God's Infinite Certainty,
He always Knows

That He is the only One
Who should ever be put on trial.

Every Movement

I rarely let the word "No" escape
From my mouth

Because it is so plain to my soul

That God has shouted, "Yes! Yes! Yes!"
To every luminous movement in Existence.

Saheb-e-Zaman

Just as a normal man can climb
A high mountain
And on a clear day
See for many miles all around,

Hafiz can stand on a blessed peak
Inside his heart
And see for hundreds of years
In all directions.

And I tell you, dear ones,
That the *Saheb-e-Zaman*,
The Christ,
The Prophet,
The Ancient One,
Has made a date to Whirl,
To Whirl
With this Earth again!

Set This Dry, Boring Place on Fire!

Hafiz seeks to broaden and deepen our understanding of "Real Love," both in human relationships and in our growing obsession with Divinity. He prods us to explore Love's possibilities and test its apparent boundaries. He says our progress on this Journey can be measured only by the intensity of our love, the living flame that illumines all life. Begin to love *now*, he says, don't wait—let there be no regrets.

"My heart is a raging volcano
Of love for you!"

How Does It Feel to Be a Heart?

Once a young woman asked me,

"How does it feel to be a man?"
And I replied,

"My dear,
I am not so sure."

Then she said,
"Well, aren't you a man?"

And this time I replied,

"I view gender
As a beautiful animal
That people often take for a walk on a leash
And might enter in some odd contest
To try to win strange prizes.

My dear,
A better question for Hafiz
Would have been,

'How does it feel to be a heart?'

For all I know is Love,
And I find my heart Infinite
And Everywhere!"

If It Is Not Too Dark

Go for a walk, if it is not too dark.
Get some fresh air, try to smile.
Say something kind
To a safe-looking stranger, if one happens by.

Always exercise your heart's knowing.

You might as well attempt something real
Along this path:

Take your spouse or lover into your arms
The way you did when you first met.
Let tenderness pour from your eyes
The way the Sun gazes warmly on the earth.

Play a game with some children.
Extend yourself to a friend.
Sing a few ribald songs to your pets and plants—
Why not let them get drunk and wild!

Let's toast
Every rung we've climbed on Evolution's ladder.
Whisper, "I love you! I love you!"
To the whole mad world.

Let's stop reading about God—
We will never understand Him.

Jump to your feet, wave your fists,
Threaten and warn the whole Universe

That your heart can no longer live
Without real love!

Awake Awhile

Awake awhile.

It does not have to be
Forever,
Right now.

One step upon the Sky's soft skirt
Would be enough.

Hafiz,
Awake awhile.
Just one True moment of Love
Will last for days.

Rest all your elaborate plans and tactics
For Knowing Him,
For they are all just frozen spring buds
Far,
So far from Summer's Divine Gold.

Awake, my dear.
Be kind to your sleeping heart.
Take it out into the vast fields of Light
And let it breathe.

Say,
"Love,
Give me back my wings.
Lift me,
Lift me nearer."

Say to the sun and moon,
Say to our dear Friend,

"I will take You up now, Beloved,
On that wonderful Dance You promised!"

Dance, Dervish Dance

Dance, dervish dance—
Bring the Face of God before you.

Only Love can lift the heart up so high
That its true Color is restored by the Sun!
See Him near and clapping,
That Perfect One who fathers Divine Rhythm.

O dance, dervish dance,
And know you bring your Master happiness
Whenever you smile.

Last night,
So many tears took flight because of Joy
That the sky got crowded and complained
When I discovered God hiding again in my heart
And I could not cease to celebrate.

O dance, Hafiz, dance.
Write a thousand luminous secrets
Upon the wall of Existence
So that even a blind man will know
Where we are,
And join us in this Love!

Dance, dervish dance—
Bring the Face,
O bring the Face of your Beloved
Before you!

You Better Start Kissing Me

Throw away
All your begging bowls at God's door,

For I have heard the Beloved
Prefers sweet threatening shouts,

Something on the order of:

"Hey, Beloved,
My heart is a raging volcano
Of love for you!

You better start kissing me—
Or Else!"

A Barroom View of Love

I would not want all my words
To parade around this world
In pretty costumes,

So I will tell you something
Of the Barroom view of Love.

Love is grabbing hold of the Great Lion's mane
And wrestling and rolling deep into Existence

While the Beloved gets rough
And begins to maul you alive.

True Love, my dear,
Is putting an ironclad grip upon

The sore, swollen balls
Of a Divine Rogue Elephant

And
Not having the good fortune to Die!

I Know the Way You Can Get

I know the way you can get
When you have not had a drink of Love:

Your face hardens,
Your sweet muscles cramp.
Children become concerned
About a strange look that appears in your eyes
Which even begins to worry your own mirror
And nose.

Squirrels and birds sense your sadness
And call an important conference in a tall tree.
They decide which secret code to chant
To help your mind and soul.

Even angels fear that brand of madness
That arrays itself against the world
And throws sharp stones and spears into
The innocent
And into one's self.

O I know the way you can get
If you have not been out drinking Love:

You might rip apart
Every sentence your friends and teachers say,
Looking for hidden clauses.

You might weigh every word on a scale
Like a dead fish.

You might pull out a ruler to measure
From every angle in your darkness
The beautiful dimensions of a heart you once
Trusted.

I know the way you can get
If you have not had a drink from Love's
Hands.

That is why all the Great Ones speak of
The vital need
To keep Remembering God,
So you will come to know and see Him
As being so Playful
And Wanting,
Just Wanting to help.

That is why Hafiz says:
Bring your cup near me,
For I am a Sweet Old Vagabond
With an Infinite Leaking Barrel
Of Light and Laughter and Truth
That the Beloved has tied to my back.

Dear one,
Indeed, please bring your heart near me.
For all I care about
Is quenching your thirst for freedom!

All a Sane man can ever care about
Is giving Love!

Spill the Oil Lamp!

Spill the oil lamp!
Set this dry, boring place on fire!

If you have ever
Made wanton love with God,

Then you have ignited that brilliant Light inside
That every person needs.

So—
Spill the oil!

I Am Determined

One regret, dear world,
That I am determined not to have
When I am lying on my deathbed
Is that
I did not kiss you enough.

Let Me Near You Tonight

Hafiz speaks of the special love a spiritual student feels for his teacher. The Master becomes the personification of Love and the focus of the student's devotion and longing. This association of spiritual student and teacher can become the most intimate and deeply personal bond of life, closer than husband and wife or parent and child. Hafiz describes the many dimensions of this relationship from the depth of his own experience with his Master.

"I need to know I am yours, Beloved."

That's the Whole Idea

Fire has a love for itself—
It wants to keep burning.

It is like a woman
Who is at last making love
To the person she most desires.

Find a Master who is like the Sun.

Go to His house
In the middle of the night.

Smash a window.
Act like a great burglar—
Jump in.

Now,
Gather all your courage—
Throw yourself into His bed!

He will probably kill you.

Fantastic—
That's the whole idea!

Keeping Watch

In the morning
When I began to wake,
It happened again—

That feeling
That You, Beloved,
Had stood over me all night
Keeping watch,

That feeling
That as soon as I began to stir

You put Your lips on my forehead
And lit a Holy Lamp
Inside my heart.

You Left a Thousand Women Crazy

Beloved,
Last time,
When You walked through the city
So Beautiful and Naked,

You left a thousand women crazy
And impossible to live with.

You left a thousand married men
Confused about their gender.

Children ran from their classrooms,
And teachers were glad You came.

And the sun tried to break out
Of its royal cage in the sky
And at last, and at last
Lay its Ancient Love at Your feet.

And I wish You would have let it,

So the whole world could have died
Like Hafiz,

Dancing so happily,
Filled with Ecstasy and
Unbearable Divine Light.

Something Invisible

Once I asked my Master,
"What is the difference
Between you and me?"

And he replied,
"Hafiz, only this:

If a herd of wild buffalo
Broke into our house
And knocked over
Our empty begging bowls,
Not a drop would spill from yours.

But there is Something Invisible
That God has placed in mine.

If That spilled from my bowl,
It could drown this whole world."

A Tethered Falcon

My heart sits on the Arm of God
Like a tethered falcon
Suddenly unhooded.

I am now blessedly crazed
Because my Master's Astounding Effulgence
Is in constant view.

My piercing eyes,
Which have searched every world
For Tenderness and Love,
Now lock on the Royal Target—
The Wild Holy One
Whose Beauty Illuminates Existence.

My soul endures a magnificent longing.

I am a tethered falcon
With great wings and sharp talons poised,
Every sinew taut, like a Sacred Bow,
Quivering at the edge of my Self
And Eternal Freedom,

Though still held in check
By a miraculous
Divine Golden Cord.

Beloved,
I am waiting for You to free me
Into Your Mind
And Infinite Being.
I am pleading in absolute helplessness
To hear, finally, your Words of Grace:
Fly! Fly into Me!

Hafiz,
Who can understand
Your sublime Nearness and Separation?

That Full, Fragrant Curl

Why do I want to get so close to you tonight,
Dear Master,
With such a sharp knife in my hand?

I'll confess.
I have been eyeing that beautiful curl dangling
At the end of your tress.

I have calculated its worth
Way into the wee hours.

I have figured
The price it will bring
Is the ransom I need to free myself
From every god my mind and this world
Have ever erected,
To free myself from every sterile idol
That makes me bow to its lies
And wants to strangle
My fragile joys and precious winged pen.

I need to know I am yours, Beloved,
To untangle my every alliance with Guilt.
When that cruel net casts itself,
It can cause even a great one
To live in sorrow and sadness.

So let me near you tonight, dear Master,
With a sharp knife concealed in my palm.
Let me cut from your favorite garment
A tiny thread
From which I will make a sacred lasso
To encircle the Sun.

If I could do *that*
With just a frayed thread,
Imagine what could happen
If you let me sever that full, fragrant curl
That holds this earth like a blue diamond ornament
Dangling from your ear.

Let it be mine,
So I might swallow at last
This tiny sacred object—this world,
That has caressed your cheek so many times.

Hafiz has learned to sing all night,
With a divine eloquence and humor,
To help fill God's artists and seekers
To the brim.

O let me near you tonight, Beloved,
With my heart concealed in my hands.
Let me near you,
And I will place it at your feet forever!

Maybe I Could Become a Poet

Hafiz sometimes speaks about himself in his poems, often in an apparently offhand and bemused way. At first he is puzzled by life. "What kind of work can I do in this world?" he asks. But the more deeply he sees, the more astonished he is to find his Beloved everywhere. He discovers that the essence of life is the expression of beauty—it is Poetry. He arrives at a stage in Love's Journey where everyone becomes a Poet!

"Start seeing everything as God,
But keep it a secret."

I Took It as a Sign

Someone sent a band to my house,
And it started playing
At five in the morning.

I took this as a sign
God wanted me to sing!

Then the moon joined in
And a few of the tenor-voiced stars,

And the earth offered its lovely belly
As a drum.

Before I knew it,
I realized
All human beings could be happy

If they just had a few music lessons
From a Sweet Old Maestro
Like Hafiz.

Beautiful Empty Pages

What kind of work
Can I do in this world?

Who would be kind enough
To hire an old holy Bum,

One with a great reputation
For loving the charms
Of the lawless
And the wild artists and the lewd?

Maybe I could become a poet.

Maybe the Beloved
Will make my love so Pure

That He will come to sit upon
All my Beautiful empty pages.
And when you come to look at them,

He might kick you
With His Beautiful Divine Foot.

Pulling Out the Chair

Pulling out the chair
Beneath your mind
And watching you fall upon God—

What else is there
For Hafiz to do
That is any fun in this world!

The Only Sin I Know

If someone sits with me
And we talk about the Beloved,

If I cannot give his heart comfort,
If I cannot make him feel better
About himself and this world,

Then, Hafiz,
Quickly run to the mosque and pray—

For you have just committed
The only sin I know.

There Is a Wonderful Game

There is a game we should play,
And it goes like this:

We hold hands and look into each other's eyes
And scan each other's face.

Then I say,
"Now tell me a difference you see between us."

And you might respond,
"Hafiz, your nose is ten times bigger than mine!"

Then I would say,
"Yes, my dear, almost ten times!"

But let's keep playing.
Let's go deeper,
Go deeper.
For if we do,
Our spirits will embrace
And interweave.

Our union will be so glorious
That even God
Will not be able to tell us apart.

There is a wonderful game
We should play with everyone
And it goes like this . . .

I Am So Glad

Start seeing everything as God,
But keep it a secret.

Become like a man who is Awestruck
And Nourished

Listening to a Golden Nightingale
Sing in a beautiful foreign language
While God invisibly nests
Upon its tongue.

Hafiz,
Who can you tell in this world
That when a dog runs up to you
Wagging its ecstatic tail,
You lean down and whisper in its ear,

"Beloved,
I am so glad You are happy to see me.

Beloved,
I am so glad,
So very glad You have come."

Your Beautiful Parched, Holy Mouth

A poet is someone
Who can pour Light into a spoon,
Then raise it
To nourish
Your beautiful parched, holy mouth.

I Will Hire You as a Minstrel

Take one of my tears,
Throw it into the ocean

And watch the salt in the wounds
Of this earth and men begin to disappear.

Take one of my tears
And cradle it in your palm.
Mount a great white camel
And carry my love into every desert,
Paying homage to every Prophet
Who has ever walked in our world.

O take one of my tears
And stop weeping only for sadness,

For there is so much More to this life
Than you now understand.

Take one of my tears
And become like the Happy One,
O like the Happy One—
Who now lives Forever
Within me.

When a drop from my Emerald Sea
Touches your soul's mouth,
It will dissolve everything but your Joy
And an Eternal Wonder.

Then,
The Beloved will gladly hire you
As His minstrel

To go traveling about this world,
Letting everyone upon this earth

Hear
The Beautiful Names of God
Resound in a thousand chords!

Hafiz himself is singing tonight
In Resplendent Glory,

For the cup in my heart
Has revealed the Beloved's Face,
And I have His oath in writing

That He will never again depart.

O Hafiz, take one of your tears,
For you are weeping like a golden candle—

Throw one tear into the Ocean of your own verse

And let the wounds
Of every lover of God who kneels in prayer
And comes close to your words
Begin, right now,
To disappear.

God's Laughter

    Hafiz tells us that the Beloved's nature is pure Joy. The closer we come to Him, the more we are able to hear and feel God's Laughter. The rhythm of His Laughter is the music of the dance of life. That music is the essence of Love, and it is the radiant core of every song of Hafiz.

"I am happy even before I have a reason."

Several Times in the Last Week

Ever since Happiness heard your name,
It has been running through the streets
Trying to find you.

And several times in the last week,
God Himself has even come to my door—
Asking me for your address!

Once I said,
"God,
I thought You knew everything.
Why are You asking me
Where Your lovers live?"

And the Beloved replied,

Indeed, Hafiz, I do know Everything—
But it is fun playing dumb once in a while.
And I love intimate chat
And the warmth of your heart's fire.

Maybe we should make this poem into a song—
I think it has potential!

How does this refrain sound,
For I know it is a Truth:

Ever since Happiness heard your name,
It has been running through the streets
Trying to find you.
And several times in the last week,
God Himself has come to my door—
So sweetly asking for your address,
Wanting the beautiful warmth of your heart's fire.

Laughter

What is laughter? What is laughter?
It is God waking up! O it is God waking up!
It is the sun poking its sweet head out
From behind a cloud
You have been carrying too long,
Veiling your eyes and heart.

It is Light breaking ground for a great Structure
That is your Real body—called Truth.

It is happiness applauding itself and then taking flight
To embrace everyone and everything in this world.

Laughter is the polestar
Held in the sky by our Beloved,
Who eternally says,

"Yes, dear ones, come this way,
Come this way toward Me and Love!

Come with your tender mouths moving
And your beautiful tongues conducting songs
And with your movements—your magic movements
Of hands and feet and glands and cells—Dancing!

Know that to God's Eye,
All movement is a Wondrous Language,
And Music—such exquisite, wild Music!"

O what is laughter, Hafiz?
What is this precious love and laughter
Budding in our hearts?

It is the glorious sound
Of a soul waking up!

Strange Miracle

O wondrous creatures,
By what strange miracle
Do you so often
Not smile?

Silence

A day of Silence
Can be a pilgrimage in itself.

A day of Silence
Can help you listen
To the Soul play
Its marvelous lute and drum.

Is not most talking
A crazed defense of a crumbling fort?

I thought we came here
To surrender in Silence,

To yield to Light and Happiness,

To Dance within
In celebration of Love's Victory!

My Sweet, Crushed Angel

You have not danced so badly, my dear,
Trying to hold hands with the Beautiful One.

You have waltzed with great style,
My sweet, crushed angel,
To have ever neared God's Heart at all.

Our Partner is notoriously difficult to follow,
And even His best musicians are not always easy
To hear.

So what if the music has stopped for a while.

So what
If the price of admission to the Divine
Is out of reach tonight.

So what, my dear,
If you do not have the ante to gamble for Real Love.

The mind and the body are famous
For holding the heart ransom,
But Hafiz knows the Beloved's eternal habits.

Have patience,

For He will not be able to resist your longing
For long.

You have not danced so badly, my dear,
Trying to kiss the Beautiful One.

You have actually waltzed with tremendous style,
O my sweet,
O my sweet, crushed angel.

Skinning Your Knees on God

Little by little,
You will turn into stars.

Even then, my dear,
You will only be
A crawling infant,
Still skinning your knees on God.

Little by little,
You will turn into
The whole sweet, amorous Universe
In heat
On a wild spring night,

And become so free
In a wonderful, secret
And pure Love
That flows
From a conscious,
One-pointed,
Infinite need for Light.

Even then, my dear,
The Beloved will have fulfilled
Just a fraction,
Just a fraction!
Of a promise
He wrote upon your heart.

When your soul begins
To Ever bloom and laugh
And spin in Eternal Ecstasy—

O little by little,
You will turn into God.

It Cuts the Plow Reins

What does Purity do?
It cuts the plow reins.

It frees you from working and dining
In the mud.

It frees you from living behind
A big ox
That is always breaking wind.

What can Purity do, my dear?

It can lift your heart
On a rising, bucking Sun
That makes the soul hunger
To reach the roof of Creation.

It offers what the whole world wants—
Real Knowledge and Power.

It offers what the wise crave—
The priceless treasure of Freedom.

Pure Divine Love is no meek priest
Or tight banker.
It will smash all your windows
And only then throw in the holy gifts.

It will allow you to befriend
Life and light and sanity—

And not even mind waking
To another day.

It reveals the excitement of the Present
And the beauty of Precision.
It confers vitality and a sublime clarity

Until finally all the heart can do
Is burst open
With great love and laughter!

O Purity,
O dear Truth and Friend within me,
Why didn't you tell me sooner
You could do all this —

Cut the reins of illusion,

So we can all
Just go wild
Loving God
And everyone all day!

A Wild, Holy Band

Your breath is a sacred clock, my dear—
Why not use it to keep time with God's Name?

And if your feet are ever mobile
Upon this ancient drum, the earth,
O do not let your precious movements
Come to naught.

Let your steps dance silently
To the rhythm of the Beloved's Name!

My fingers and my hands
Never move through empty space,
For there are
Invisible golden lute strings all around,
Sending Resplendent Chords
Throughout the Universe.

I hear the voice
Of every creature and plant,
Every world and sun and galaxy—
Singing the Beloved's Name!

I have awakened to find violin and cello,
Flute, harp and trumpet,
Cymbal, bell and drum—
All within me!
From head to toe, every part of my body
Is chanting and clapping!

Hafiz,
The Beloved has made you
Such a Luminous Man!

For with constant remembrance of God,
One's whole body will become
A Wonderful and Wild,
Holy Band!

Forever Dance

I am happy even before I have a reason.

I am full of Light even before the sky
Can greet the sun or the moon.

Dear companions,
We have been in love with God
For so very, very long.

What can Hafiz now do but Forever
Dance!

The Life and Work of Hafiz

by Henry S. Mindlin, Consulting Editor

Despite the popularity of Hafiz in the East, reliable information about the details of his life is sketchy. Scholars do not even agree about his dates of birth and death. He was probably born about 1320 and died about 1388-89, roughly the same dates as the first great poet who wrote in English, Geoffrey Chaucer. His given name was Shams-ud-din Muhammad. He chose the name Hafiz ("memorizer") as a pen name when he began to write poetry; it is a title given to someone who knows the entire Quran by heart, as he apparently did. Hafiz was born in Shiraz, a beautiful city in southern Persia that escaped the ravages of the Mongol and Tartar invasions during this violent and chaotic period of history. He spent nearly all of his life in this cultured garden city.

Early Life

All is written within the Mind
To help and instruct the dervish
In dance and romance and prayer.

Hafiz did not have an easy or comfortable life. He was the youngest of three sons of poor parents. His father was a coal merchant who died when Hafiz was in his teens. To help support the family, Hafiz worked as a baker's assistant by day and put himself through school at night, using part of his salary to pay his tuition. Over many years, he mastered the subjects of a "classical" medieval education: Quranic law and theology, grammar, mathematics and astronomy. He also mastered calligraphy, which in the centuries before printing was a highly refined art form. Islamic calligraphy was originally developed as a sacred art to preserve and glorify the Quran, the message of God. Since representational art was forbidden by religious law, calligraphy reached a remarkable degree of subtlety and expressiveness. Hafiz was a skilled draftsman and occasionally worked as a professional copyist.

His early education naturally included the great Persian poets: Saadi of Shiraz, Farid-ud-din Attar, Jalal-ud-din Rumi and others. Poetry is a national art in Persia, somewhat like opera in Italy. Even in modern Iran, people at every social level know the great poets, argue passionately about their favorites and quote them constantly in everyday conversation. In medieval Persia, the art of poetry was taken seriously and valued highly. Local princes and provincial governors employed court poets to create epic verses celebrating their greatness. When the ruler was especially pleased by a composition, the poet was sometimes placed on a scale and rewarded with his weight in gold.

Court Poet

A poet is someone
Who can pour Light into a Spoon.

Hafiz had a natural poetic gift. Even as a child, he was able to improvise poems on any subject in any form and style. When he was in his early twenties, some of his love poems began to circulate in Shiraz, and he was soon invited to participate in poetry gatherings at court. He won the patronage of a succession of rulers and wealthy noblemen. One of his benefactors founded a religious college and offered Hafiz a position as a teacher. Thus, during his middle years, he served as a court poet and a college professor. He married and had at least one son.

Hafiz's livelihood depended solely on patronage. Everyone admired his literary brilliance, but his poetry boldly celebrated ideas that bordered on heresy, and he had enemies among the rigorously orthodox who "blacklisted" him whenever they came to power. Periodically, he would fall out of favor and lose his position, both at court and in the college. He could sometimes use his skills as a copyist to support his family until his fortunes improved. At least once, however, he was forced to leave Shiraz. For several years he lived as an exile, often in dire poverty. Finally a new, more tolerant regime allowed him to return home and resume his career. During the long, unsettled middle period of his life, first his son and later his wife passed away. Some scholars associate many of his deeply felt verses of grief, separation and loss with these events.

By the time he was sixty, Hafiz had become famous as a master poet. A circle of students and companions gathered around him, and he served them as a teacher and counselor until his quiet death at about the age of seventy. He was buried in one of his favorite spots, at the foot of a cypress tree he himself had planted in a rose garden near Shiraz. For five hundred years his tomb, surrounded by the rose garden, was a center of pilgrimage and refreshment for thousands. By the early twentieth century, however, the tomb had fallen into disrepair. Then in 1925, arrangements were made with the Persian government to have a new structure built over the grave and to have the gardens gradually restored. These arrangements were initiated and partially funded by a contemporary spiritual figure from India who loved Hafiz, Avatar Meher Baba. This modern world teacher frequently quoted couplets of Hafiz to illustrate his own discussions of spiritual principles. Meher Baba explained that the love poetry of Hafiz contained all the secrets of the spiritual path —for the true subject matter of spirituality is Love.

Spiritual Student

We have been in love with God
For so very, very long.

Hafiz was, in fact, a spiritual student. As a young man, he became a disciple of a Sufi teacher who guided him through a difficult spiritual apprenticeship that lasted most of his adult life. Later, Hafiz himself became a Sufi master. His *Divan* (collected poems) is a classic in the literature of Sufism, an ancient spiritual tradition whose special emphasis is intense, often ecstatic, one-pointed devotion to God.

In the West, Sufism is usually regarded as a form of Islamic mysticism. However, the Sufis themselves say their "way" has always existed, under many names, in many lands, associated with the mystical dimension of every spiritual system. In ancient Greece, for example, they were identified with the wisdom *(sophia)* schools of Pythagoras and Plato. At the time of Jesus, they were called Essenes or Gnostics. After Muhammad, they adopted many of the principles and formulations of Islam and became known in the Muslim world as "Sufis," a word given various meanings, including "wisdom," "purity" and "wool" (for the coarse woolen habits of wandering dervishes).

From about 800 to 1400 A.D., Sufi schools flourished under the guidance of master teachers such as Rumi and Ibn Arabi. As individual schools developed, their methods of teaching diversified according to the needs of each group. Some stressed formal meditation, others focused on selfless service to the world, and still others emphasized devotional practices: song, dance and spiritual poetry celebrating love for God. The Sufis cherish the poetry of Hafiz as a perfect expression of the human experience of divine love.

How Hafiz came to be a Sufi student is a famous and popular story told in many versions throughout the East:

It is said that when he was twenty-one and working as a baker's assistant, Hafiz delivered some bread to a mansion and happened to catch a fleeting glimpse of a beautiful girl on the terrace. That one glimpse captured his heart, and he fell madly in love with her, though she did not even notice him. She was from a wealthy noble family, and he was a poor baker's assistant. She was beautiful, he was short and physically unattractive—the situation was hopeless.

As months went by, Hafiz made up poems and love songs celebrating her beauty and his longing for her. People heard him singing his poems and began to repeat them; the poems were so touching that they became popular all over Shiraz.

Hafiz was oblivious of his new fame as a poet; he thought only of his beloved. Desperate to win her, he undertook an arduous spiritual discipline that required him to keep a vigil at the tomb of a certain saint all night long for forty nights. It was said that anyone who could accomplish this near-impossible austerity would be granted his heart's desire. Every day Hafiz went to work at the bakery. Every night he went to the saint's tomb and willed himself to stay awake for love of this girl. His love was so strong that he succeeded in completing this vigil.

At daybreak on the fortieth day, the archangel Gabriel appeared before Hafiz and told him to ask for whatever he wished. Hafiz had never seen such a glorious, radiant being as Gabriel. He found himself thinking, "If God's messenger is so beautiful, how much more beautiful must God be!" Gazing on the unimaginable splendor of God's angel, Hafiz forgot all about the girl, his wish, everything. He said, "I want God!"

Gabriel then directed Hafiz to a spiritual teacher who lived in Shiraz. The angel told Hafiz to serve this teacher in every way and his wish would be fulfilled. Hafiz hurried to meet his teacher, and they began their work together that very day.

Hafiz and His Teacher

Our Partner is notoriously difficult to follow,
And even His best musicians are not always easy
To hear.

The teacher's name was Muhammad Attar. "Attar" signifies a chemist or perfumer, and it is believed that Muhammad Attar owned a shop in Shiraz and lived a very ordinary public life. Only his small circle of students knew him as a spiritual teacher.

Hafiz visited Attar nearly every day for years. They sat together, sometimes dined together, sometimes talked, sometimes sang, sometimes went for quiet walks in the beautiful rose gardens of Shiraz. Attar opened Hafiz's vision to fresh, ever deeper perceptions of the beauty and harmony of life and a much broader understanding of all the processes of love. It was natural for Hafiz to express these insights in the language of poetry. Muhammad Attar was also a poet, and he encouraged Hafiz in this direction. For many years, Hafiz created a poem a day for his teacher. Attar told his students to collect and study these poems, for they illustrated many of the central principles of spiritual unfolding.

However, the relationship between Hafiz and his teacher was not always an easy one. In many accounts, Muhammad Attar is presented as a stern and demanding figure who sometimes appeared to show no compassion at all for Hafiz. Modern spiritual figures, notably Avatar Meher Baba, have used the example of Hafiz and Attar to illustrate how challenging and difficult it can be to serve an authentic spiritual teacher. In his discourses on the role of the master, Meher Baba explains that, regardless of external appearances, a teacher must always aid internal processes of growth that support increasingly broader designs of love. Along the way, the student's limited ego is dissolved—or as Hafiz says, ground to dust. Meher Baba described this process as "hell on earth" for Hafiz. He said, "Hafiz, so to speak, broke his head at the feet of his master," day after day, year after year, for forty long years.

Some stories about Hafiz and his teacher support this view. Often Hafiz is portrayed as running to Attar in despair, pleading for enlightenment or spiritual liberation after decades of frustration. Each time, Attar would tell Hafiz to be patient and wait, and all would be revealed. According to one account:

One day, when Hafiz was well over sixty, he confronted his aged teacher and said, "Look at me! I'm old, my wife and son are long dead. What have I gained by being your obedient disciple for all these years?" Attar gently replied, "Be patient and one day you will know." Hafiz shouted, "I knew I would get that answer from you!" In a fever of spiritual desperation, he began another form of forty-day vigil. This time he drew a circle on the ground and sat within it for forty days and nights, without leaving it for food, drink or even to relieve himself. On the fortieth day, the angel again appeared to him and asked what he desired. Hafiz discovered that during the forty days all his desires had disappeared. He replied instantly that his only wish was to serve his teacher.

Just before dawn Hafiz came out of the circle and went to his teacher's house. Attar was waiting at the door. They embraced warmly, and Attar gave Hafiz a special cup of aged wine. As they drank together, the intoxicating joy of the wine opened his heart and dissolved every trace of separateness. With a great laugh of delight, Hafiz was forever drowned in love and united with God, his divine Beloved.

It is said that Hafiz unknowingly began his vigil *exactly* forty days before the end of his fortieth year of service to his teacher and that the "moment of union" was *exactly* forty years to the day from the moment they first met.

Levels of Love

All I know is Love,
And I find my heart Infinite
And Everywhere!

Many of these vignettes about Hafiz have the charming symmetry and precision of symbolic teaching stories. The recurring number forty, for example, might not be meant literally. In spiritual literature, "forty" is often used to indicate a term of learning or change, such as the "forty days and forty nights" of Noah's Flood. Forty is also called "the number of perseverance," marking a period of growth through testing, trial and purification. After the exodus from Egypt, the Israelites endured "forty years of wandering" in the wilderness before they were ready to enter the Promised Land. Jesus, following the ancient practice of the prophets, went into the desert for a great seclusion of forty days, which he described as a period of purification and preparation for the next stage of his work. The Buddha attained final enlightenment after forty days of continuous meditation. One can find many examples, East and West.

These tales of Hafiz share other common symbols. There is the "mystic circle," which is an image of completion or perfection. And there is the glass of wine Attar gives Hafiz. A glass or cup is a vessel, which can often represent the human heart, or even the human being as a vessel of love. "Wine" stands for love in many spiritual traditions. Aged wine, such as Attar shares with Hafiz, can represent the purified (distilled) essence of knowing or love.

As teaching stories, these episodes can be seen to illustrate central stages of the Sufi "path of love" or inner unfolding:

Hafiz begins his spiritual journey as nearly everyone does — he is awakened to love. An ideal of human beauty and perfection seizes his heart. Desperate to win his ideal, he fully explores the realm of human love *(his poems and songs celebrate her beauty and his longing for her)*.

Finally, he directs all the energies of his life to the pursuit of love *(a forty-day vigil)*.

When his longing reaches its highest pitch *(dawn of the final day)*, a new and higher dimension of love reveals itself *(Gabriel)*. He is able to respond to the beauty of this higher understanding *("I want God!")*, and his response ushers him into a new phase of learning and a new relationship of love *(with a spiritual teacher)*.

This new term of growth *(forty years)* is exponentially longer than the first one. Attar leads Hafiz through a review of increasingly broader and more encompassing levels of love *(a poem a day)*. Hafiz becomes restless as his love for God grows stronger. Attar constantly counsels "patience" to remind Hafiz that every stage of love must be fully explored, honored and lived.

As the term nears its end, Hafiz reaches a new height of desperation and longing for his Beloved. He again seeks to devote all his energies to love *(another forty-day vigil)*. This time he binds himself within a circle *(of perfection or completion)*, literally circumscribing all his thoughts and actions to a single focus—God. He strives to perfect his love for God until nothing else exists for him.

When he has truly accomplished this *(dawn of the final day)*, he finds that the force of love has consumed his limited personality and all its desires, even the desire for God. He has realized that one cannot "master" love, one can only serve as a vessel of love *(a glass of wine)*.

Emerging from the circle, Hafiz is now able to approach and embrace every experience of life with the unlimited wisdom of love *(he and his teacher embrace)*. He and Attar now share the same perfect knowing *(the aged wine of love's maturity)*. The "glass of aged wine" now becomes a symbol for "the embodiment of perfect love"—Hafiz himself.

Perfection

I hear the voice
Of every creature and plant,
Every world and sun and galaxy—
Singing the Beloved's Name!

The idea that a human being can achieve "perfect love" or "perfect knowing" may seem extraordinary, yet it is a belief shared by most spiritual systems. It is called by many names— "union with the Father," *"nirvikalpa samadhi,"* "the highest development of consciousness," "God-realization," *"Qutubiyat"* or simply "Perfection." One who attains it can be called a Perfect Master, someone who embodies a perfect understanding of the beauty and harmony of the universe.

A Perfect Master experiences life as an infinite and continuous flow of divine love, swirling in, around and through all forms of life and all realms of creation. It is an experience of total unity with all life and all beings. A Perfect Master personifies perfect joy, perfect knowing and perfect love and expresses these qualities in every activity of life.

In the Western world, the most familiar example of such perfect love may be St. Francis of Assisi. In the East, there have been many—Rumi in Persia, Kabir and Ramakrishna in India, Milarepa in Tibet, Lao-tzu in China are all revered as Perfect Masters.[1]

The teacher of Hafiz, Muhammad Attar, was a Perfect Master, and so was Hafiz himself. The poetry of Hafiz can be read as a record of a human being's journey to perfect joy, perfect knowing and perfect love.

---

[1] World Teachers such as Jesus, Buddha, Krishna and Muhammad also exemplify perfection.

Master Poet

Write a thousand luminous secrets
Upon the wall of Existence
So that even a blind man will know
Where we are,
And join us in this Love!

Hafiz developed his poetry under the guidance of his teacher. Muhammad Attar reviewed and discussed the poems in his teaching circle, and many of them were set to music. This was a common practice in Sufi schools of the time, including Rumi's order of "whirling dervishes" in Turkey. Poetry and song, easy to memorize and repeat, were used as teaching materials to encapsulate or summarize spiritual principles. With Attar's encouragement, Hafiz perfected this teaching method using a popular form of love song, the *ghazal.* He wrote hundreds of *ghazals,* finding ways to bring new depth and meaning to the lyrics without losing the accustomed association of a love song.

His poems expressed every nuance and stage of his growing understanding of love. He wrote of the game of love, the beauty of the Beloved, the sweet pain of longing, the agony of waiting, the ecstatic joy of union. He explored different forms and levels of love: his delight in nature's beauty, his romantic courtship of that ideal, unattainable girl, his sweet affection for his wife, his tender feelings for his child—and his terrible grief and loneliness when, later in his life, both his wife and his son passed away. He wrote of his relationship with his teacher and his adoration of God.

All who heard his poetry could easily associate it with their own most cherished experiences of love. The familiar rhythms of the love song, the *ghazal,* made the poems easy to learn. Before long, his poems were sung all over Persia by people from every walk of life—farmers, craftsmen, scholars, princes, even children.

Many who knew of Hafiz and enjoyed his poetry had no idea that he was a Sufi. Nor did many people know the spiritual status of his teacher. Like many Sufi masters of his time, Muhammad Attar met with his students in secret, and Hafiz did not reveal his own association with Attar until after his master's death. In the religious climate of medieval Persia, this secrecy was essential. From time to time, waves of what might be called fanatical fundamentalism swept through the country. To these fundamentalists, it was blasphemy to suggest that any human being could attain perfection or approach direct knowledge of divinity. The Sufi schools were frequently outlawed, and many of their adherents were tried and executed. Those who survived were forced to meet in secret and disguise their teachings in a symbolic language that would not offend the orthodox. This became the language of Sufi poetry. Images of wine and the Tavern came to represent love and the Sufi school; the nightingale and the Rose were the lover and the Beloved. Spiritual students were depicted as clowns, beggars, scoundrels, rogues, courtesans or intoxicated wayfarers.

This symbolic language developed gradually over hundreds of years. Hafiz brought it to perfection in his poetry. Even today, people argue about the "true" meaning of his verses—is he simply describing the joy of walking in the garden or speaking symbolically about God's delight in the material forms of His Creation? Or both? When he praises a wealthy patron or the charms of a young woman, is he really celebrating God, his true Patron and Beloved? Perhaps both. For Hafiz does not see God as separate from the world— wherever there is love, there is the Beloved. The Indian Sufi teacher Inayat Khan explained, "The mission of Hafiz was to express to a fanatical religious world that the presence of God is not to be found only in heaven, but also here on earth."

In Persian, Hafiz is sometimes called "The Tongue of the Invisible," for so many of his poems seem to be ecstatic and beautiful love songs from God to His beloved world. Hafiz shares his intoxication with the magic and beauty of divine life that pulsates everywhere around us and within us. He scorns hypocrisy and mediocrity and urges us to rise on the wings of love. He challenges us to confront and master the strongest forces of our own nature. He encourages us to celebrate even the most ordinary experiences of life as precious divine gifts. He invites us to "awake awhile" and listen to the delightful music of God's laughter.

> *What is this precious love and laughter*
> *Budding in our hearts?*
> *It is the glorious sound*
> *Of a soul waking up!*

Select Bibliography

Daniel Ladinsky

Those interested in exploring more of the life and work of Hafiz will find much information and many different approaches to the poems in the following books, which have been helpful to me:

The *Divan*

The Divan-i-Hafiz. Translated into English prose by Lieut.-Col. H. Wilberforce Clarke. 2 vols. 1891. Reprint, New York: Samuel Weiser, 1970.

This is the literal translation I have found most helpful in my own work. (I have a "deluxe" edition of the reprint, issued in Iran.) Clarke's 44-page preface summarizes the life of Hafiz and gives an outline of sources.

Divan of Hafiz. English version by Paul Smith. 2 vols. Melbourne: New Humanity Books, 1986.

The contemporary Australian poet Paul Smith has written a version of all 791 poems attributed to Hafiz. He worked for many years to duplicate or simulate as closely as possible in English the rhyme scheme and meter of every one of Hafiz's poems. The result is the second volume of this set. In the first volume, a separate 256-page book, Mr. Smith has assembled what may be the most comprehensive collection of information and legends about Hafiz, his life and times and his poetry. This first volume contains an enormous Hafiz bibliography and a fascinating study of the history of Hafiz scholarship and translation in the West, including some intriguing quotes about Hafiz and his poetry by Goethe, Ralph Waldo Emerson, Edward Fitzgerald (best known for his version of the *Rubaiyat* of Omar Khayyam), the Sufi teacher Hazrat Inayat Khan and many others. Emerson said, "Hafiz defies you to show him or put him in a condition inopportune or ignoble. . . . He fears nothing. He sees too far; he sees throughout; such is the only man I wish to see or be."

Selected Poems

Arberry, Arthur J., comp. *Fifty Poems of Hafiz*. 1953. Reprint, Richmond, Surrey, UK: Curzon Press, 1993.

This paperback anthology presents poems by 15 translators. It may be the most accessible book of Hafiz's poetry currently available in America. It contains an excellent 34-page introduction and some 50 pages of scholarly notes. The poems are printed in both English and Persian.

Bell, Gertrude Lowthian, trans. *Teachings of Hafiz*. 1897. Reprint, with a preface by E. Denison Ross and introduction by Idries Shah, London: Octagon Press, 1979.

Gertrude Bell's 43 translations of Hafiz were considered some of the best of the nineteenth century. She supplements her rhymed versions with detailed notes about individual lines and phrases. This edition also includes 90 pages of informative essays by the Sufi author Idries Shah, the Oriental scholar E. Denison Ross, and a long translator's preface by Miss Bell.

Kennedy, Maud. *The Immortal Hafiz*. North Myrtle Beach, SC: Manifestation, 1987.

This delightful small volume is a free rendering that draws heavily from a translation of Hafiz by John Payne published privately in London in 1901. John Payne was a member of the Persia Society of London, as was John M. Watkins, whose translation is cited below. Mr. Payne was also a friend of H. Wilberforce Clarke and is believed to have collaborated on Clarke's translation mentioned above.

Nakosteen, Mehdi. *The Ghazaliyyat of Haafez of Shiraz*. Boulder, Colorado: Este Es Press, 1973.

Free translations from Persian to English of 124 poems. This 370-page hardbound volume by a distinguished Persian scholar, a professor at the University of Colorado, contains 37 pages of interesting introductory material and notes. The poems are printed in both English and Persian.

Watkins, John M. *Selections from the Rubaiyat and Odes of Hafiz, Together with an Account of Sufi Mysticism*. 1920. Reprint, London: Stuart and Watkins, 1970.

An informative 40-page preface discusses central themes in the poetry and includes a glossary of Sufi technical terms.

The "Path of Love" and Inner Unfolding

In the past twenty years, dozens of books have been published in English about the "classical" Sufism of Hafiz's time. However, the sources I have found most helpful in understanding the spirituality of Hafiz are the contemporary works of Avatar Meher Baba. His books give the clearest presentation of spiritual principles I have ever seen. And to underline his points, he quotes Hafiz (in his own direct translations) throughout his works. Of his many writings, I would recommend the following:

Meher Baba. *Discourses.* 7th ed. Myrtle Beach, SC: Sheriar Press, 1987.

This wonderful 433-page paperback volume is a collection of dozens of short essays on issues of spiritual life. Meher Baba discusses the spiritual path, stages of love and processes of internal development. He gives a detailed review of the work of a spiritual master and the complexities of the master-disciple relationship. He also addresses what might be called "practical mysticism" as it applies to everyday life.

Meher Baba. *God Speaks: The Theme of Creation and Its Purpose.* 2nd ed., revised and enlarged. New York: Dodd, Mead, 1973.

Meher Baba's primary work on the structure and purpose of creation and the evolution, involution and perfection of consciousness. There are many charts and diagrams and a long Supplement that includes many quotes from Hafiz to illustrate different stages of the spiritual path. Since its perspective is so vast, it is not an easy book to start with, but it is rewarding to study and contemplate.

About the Author

DANIEL LADINSKY was born in St. Louis, Missouri, in 1948. In his teens he began a spiritual quest that led him around the world. He was especially drawn to India, a land he visits regularly. For six years, Mr. Ladinsky made his home in a small spiritual community in western India, where he was given the rare privilege of living with the close companions *(mandali)* of Avatar Meher Baba, the preeminent spiritual figure of this age. While staying with the mandali, he began his work with Hafiz, Meher Baba's favorite poet. Mr. Ladinsky now resides in a small town on the South Carolina coast where he continues his work with Hafiz.